OPTICAL ILLUSIONS
AND THE VISUAL ARTS

c. 3

OPTICAL ILLUSIONS AND THE VISUAL ARTS

Ronald G. Carraher   Jacqueline B. Thurston

VAN NOSTRAND REINHOLD COMPANY/NEW YORK   STUDIO VISTA LIMITED/LONDON

Copyright © 1966 by Litton Educational Publishing, Inc.

Library of Congress Catalog Card Number 66-24549
ISBN 0-442-11174-6

Layout by Ronald G. Carraher and Jacqueline B. Thurston

Published in the United States by
Van Nostrand Reinhold Company,
450 West 33rd Street, New York, N.Y. 10001
and in Great Britain by
Studio Vista Limited,
Blue Star House, Highgate Hill, London N.19

16 15 14 13 12 11 10 9 8 7 6 5

pg 126

CONTENTS

PREFACE

The works of art reproduced in this book define some of the ways in which an artist may express his interest in perceptual effects and optical illusions. The means that he uses to create his statements are examined in their role as a determinant of the viewer's visual reactions. Some tentative explanations for specific illusions are offered; however, since a great many questions about the "seeing" process remain unanswered, no thorough scientific treatment of the subject is attempted.

Historical beginnings are a separate topic, but some early works of special interest are included. Most of the reproductions represent the work of contemporary artists, and were chosen for variety, interest, and value in explicating the formal range of style and attitudes. Although the subject is related to such areas as architecture, interior design, theatre set design, fashion design, packaging and motion picture animation, the numerous applications of perceptual ideas are only partially documented in this context. With few exceptions the works reproduced were originally executed in black and white. Works employing color were included only if they retained sufficient clarity in achromatic form. Conceptually related resources and traditional optical diagrams have been organized in a glossary that forms the conclusion.

The contents of this book are intended to broaden the concept of optical or geometric art. The reader's visual pleasure and his increased interest in his own perceptual process will fulfill our purpose.

Ronald G. Carraher
Jacqueline B. Thurston

INTRODUCTION

The optical illusion is traditionally defined as a visual experience in which a discrepancy exists between our perceptual judgment and the actual physical character of the original stimulus. An involvement in the "seeing" process develops as the viewer becomes intellectually aware of the disparity between subjective information and objective fact.

The most direct utilization of optical illusions and perceptual abstraction in a work of art occurs without recourse to association, symbol, or recognizable subject matter. The artist working with optical forms confronts the viewer with a design that will elicit a predictable visual reaction. This puristic intention most clearly reveals the character and quality of optical effects. Terms such as *retinal experience, visual reaction, perceptual abstraction,* and *optical effect* all contribute some feeling of the broader meaning that "optical illusion" will have in this context.

When used in conjunction with recognizable imagery or a representational style, the role of the illusion is modified. The viewer's reaction becomes the product of expectation, prior experience, and the innate tendency to trust certain visual cues.

The artist has relied primarily upon trial and error, careful observation, and introspection into his own perceptual process in developing a working vocabulary of optical forms. Though contributions from scientific areas have been a source of information for the artist it is the scientist who has more often investigated the properties of art.

We take pleasure in being visually deceived and we often choose to subject our senses to special kinds of optical stimulation. We delight in disturbing and testing the outer limits of visual tension and balance. We enjoy reflecting on our own mental and visual processes as they become an extension of a work of art.

9

1 PERCEPTUAL EFFECTS

A number of basic forms are used in optical art to produce specific visual reactions in the viewer. These forms serve as a visual vocabulary for the artist and function as perceptual models for the more memorable designs of the finished work of art. Some of the perceptual effects most commonly used in painting, photography, and graphic design are grouped together in this section. The resource value of these three categories considered individually depends upon the intent and the inventiveness of the artist.

The binary language for many of the painters and designers working with optical effects is black and white. Their indivisible character provides a particularly dramatic vehicle for a wide range of perceptual experiences. A direct connection exists between the purity of value contrasts and the clarity of form needed for maximum sensory impact. Black and white function optically somewhat like complementary colors because they present the eye with extremes of retinal stimulation. As the visual system is fatigued the eye fluctuates to sustain a consistent image. This process of adaptation may produce a sense of overlapping or shifting images. Black and white vibration is an important aspect of most of the perceptual effects presented in this section.

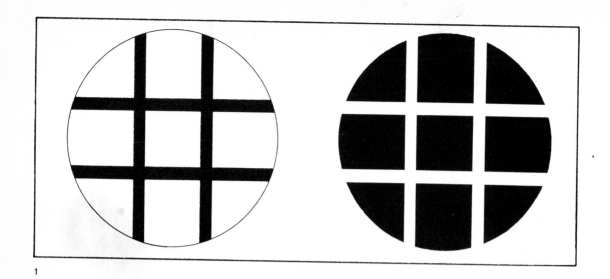

1

NEGATIVE AFTERIMAGES

Retinal fatigue is one causal factor for the phenomenon of negative afterimages. As the viewer gazes steadily at high contrast black and white figures small grey spots begin to appear on the intersections of the crosses (1). Staring intently first at a white cross on a black background and then at a blank white wall will also result in a black negative afterimage.

BRIGHTNESS CONTRAST

The eye discriminates differences between shades of grey in terms of relative brightness. A given area is judged light or dark as it is compared with an adjacent area of darker or lighter values. Areas equal in value will be consistently judged unequal if they are viewed against contrasting reference backgrounds (2).

IRRADIATION

A brightly illuminated white area is thought to produce an image on the retina that "spreads" or affects the receptors of the eye in a less selective way than by a black or dark grey image. This spreading effect may account for the illusion that black and white areas of equal size appear unequal (3).

LIGHTING DIRECTION

Conditioning prepares the eye to interpret the shadows on a three-dimensional form resulting from an overhead source of light. If this direction of illumination is reversed or the shadow pattern is inverted, a convex form may suddenly appear concave (4).

2

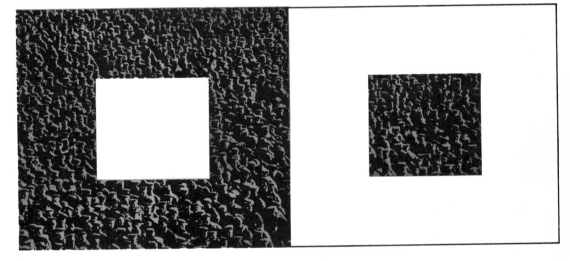

3

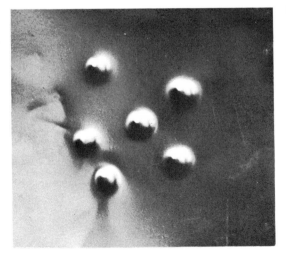

4

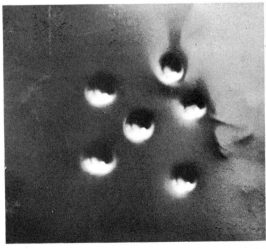

6

PATTERN AND PERIODIC STRUCTURES

A number of perceptual effects can be developed within the format of a uniform geometric pattern. The pattern or periodic structure may consist of simple elements such as triangles, circles, diamonds, or even repeated letterforms. If the individual units of the pattern are small enough or are viewed at a distance they may fuse to produce a single value in the same way that the grey of a newspaper photograph is created by a pattern of black and white dots (6).

When the units are large enough to be perceived separately, they tend to connect and regroup according to their shape and the fluctuation of the viewer's attention (5). Systematic variations of either the shape, direction, size, number, or value of the serialized units can result in pulsation, warping, and related illusions of movement. The scale of the units and the viewing distance are important determinants of the quality of the effect.

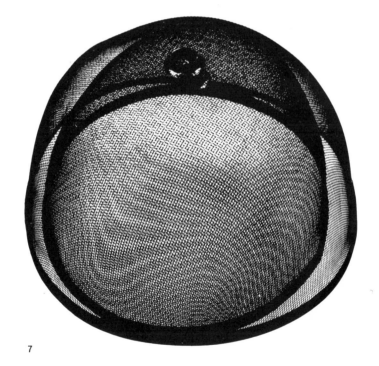

7

8

9

MOIRÉ

The term *moiré* is used to describe the dramatic structures which emerge when two or more similar geometric patterns of periodic units are overlapped (8)(9). The effect of the moiré pattern is most pronounced if the spacing between the repetitive elements in each pattern is nearly equal and the angle of intersection between the two patterns is small. An exhaustive exploration of the phenomenon has been undertaken by the physicist Gerald Oster. His studies provide partial clues which help to explain the basis of the moiré effect. Oster places special emphasis on the points of intersection of the superimposed grids: "Apparently the eye is unable to resolve the intersection. When many parallel lines cross, as in the case of two overlapped grids, the eye unconsciously searches the field and ties together these preferred points of intersection."

Two metal screen food covers have been stacked to produce an example of the moiré pattern (7).

10   Ronald C. James. *Dalmatian Dog*. 1966. Courtesy the photographer.

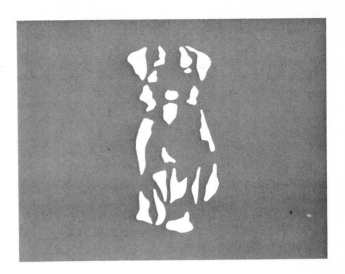

11

12

CLOSURE

Closure describes the perceptual tendency to fill in gaps or spaces which may exist in an incomplete visual pattern. Closure is experienced at the moment when a group of separate and disjointed shapes is suddenly understood as part of a larger visual form or recognizable subject (11). The realization is often so instantaneous that the new meaning seems unrelated to the preliminary study of the figure. As the viewer's perceptual skills develop, fewer and fewer visual cues are required to achieve closure.

The protective coloration of an animal illustrates how a camouflaged figure may relate to the closure principle (12). If sufficient visual information is obscured or distorted, one image may seem imbedded in another. The identifiable outline of a Dalmatian dog disappears when its markings merge in an environment of light and shadow (10). Military applications of camouflage are similarly involved in concealing a specific shape by covering it with a distracting configuration or pattern.

13   Newspaper advertisement (detail). *Stuttgarter Nachrichten*. Design: Herbert Kapitzki. Courtesy the designer.

14

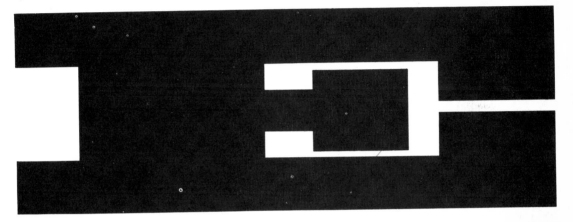

15

FIGURE-GROUND

Figure-ground refers to our capacity to distinguish or separate an object from its general environment. Numerous factors such as size, shape, value, and closure may determine which pieces of information will be perceived as figure and which will become the subordinate ground. Figure generally has a shape or object quality, and seems to exist in front of the ground.

Some figure-ground statements may be experienced as equivocal or reversible relationships. The visual impact is achieved when the eye cannot choose between the positive and negative shapes and is forced to repeatedly shift from one area to the other (13). Typographical designers of the late 19th century created alphabets that utilized the full power of this optical effect, but as early as 1840 Wells and Webb used this device in creating their alphabet in Antique Extended (15). Any black and white stripe pattern with nearly equal divisions is potentially a reversible figure-ground event. The Greek key motif or meander, with its interlocking black and white bands, provides an example of the reversible figure-ground (14).

16   Victor Vasarely. *Pleione*. 1961-63. 79³/₄ x 83³/₄". Courtesy Pace Gallery, New York.

INTERRUPTED SYSTEMS

Patterns and periodic systems such as checkerboard squares, stripes, and gradients can be altered to produce a variety of spatial illusions. Systematically enlarging or reducing the elements of select areas of the pattern can create a sense of surface magnification or swelling (16). If the pattern is cut and shifted along certain lines of interruption the result may be an apparent spatial relocation of the new shapes and planes (18). When the individual units of a sufficiently delicate pattern are modified, changes in value occur, and a sense of space is created through diminished dark-light contrast (17).

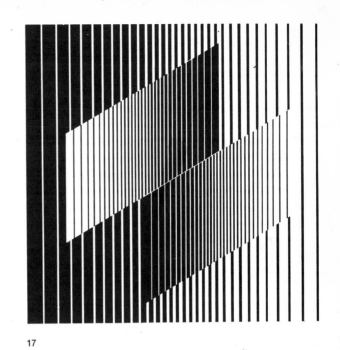

17

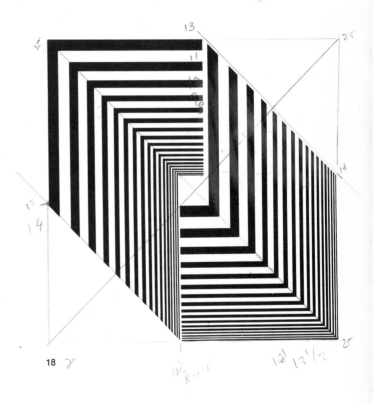

18

19   American box quilt. 1860. Silk and satin patchwork, 77½ x 77½". Collection Brooklyn Museum, New York.

20   Mosaic from the house of Menander at Antioch. III century A.D. Courtesy the Committee for the Excavation of Antioch and Its Vicinity.

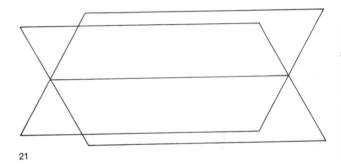

21

REVERSIBLE GEOMETRIC FIGURES

Certain geometric figures create a retinal picture or pattern of stimulation which evokes a sense of three-dimensional space on a two-dimensional surface. It is uncertain whether the capacity to perceive this illusion, with the assistance of specific cues, is innate in vision or is the product of conditioned seeing. Converging lines, oblique sets of parallel lines, overlapping planes, and location in the visual field are among the techniques used by the artist to indicate the third dimension. Linear perspective and isometric drawing are systems that incorporate these devices. When a geometric figure contains two sets of contradictory spatial cues, the figure tends to reverse its position in space as our attention shifts from one set of cues to the other (21).

Roman floor tiles and the pieces of cloth in a patchwork quilt form designs that document man's persisting interest and pleasure in reversible figures (20) (19).

22

23

26

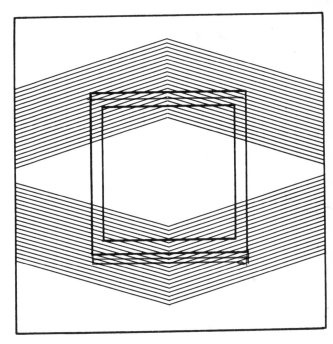

24

ILLUSIONS OF SIZE AND DIRECTION

Learning, habits of seeing, and the physiological process of perception contribute to certain errors in our attempts to judge size and direction. Illusions of direction involve a discrepancy between measurable fact and visual appearance. Such illusions range from fairly simple line figures to complex superimposed patterns. An environment of strong directional forces may disrupt the form of a simple geometric figure (23). The resultant illusion is in part the consequence of our inability to separate the figure from its environment. Two familiar illusions of this type are the basis for the adjacent figures. Verticals consistently appear longer than horizontals of equal length (22). Straight lines seem to bend as they cross a background grid of intersecting diagonals (24). Numerous variations of illusions of size and direction may be found in the glossary.

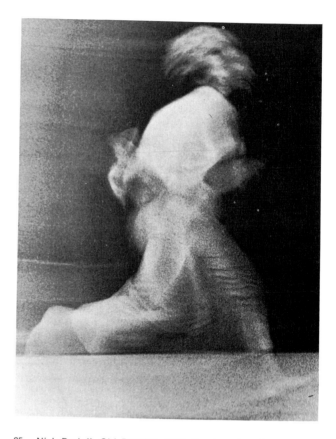

25   Nick Pavloff. *Girl Running.* 1964. Courtesy the photographer.

DIFFUSION OF EDGE

Accommodation refers to the shape adjustment mechanism of the lens of the eye as it focuses an image on the retina. When the boundaries of an edge are diffused or partially blurred, tension is created as the eye unsuccessfully attempts to accommodate itself to the indistinct form (25). The visual frustration is heightened if the texture and scale of the diffused edge are sufficiently refined. A variety of effects may be employed to produce this edge quality, each of which functions at a slightly different optimum distance. Because the eye shifts and explores the figure in an attempt to resolve the ambiguity, there is a relationship between actual movement and this static illusion. Our previous experience with the indistinct edge of a fast-moving object demonstrates that the diffusion of edge serves as a stimulus toward movement, as well as a symbol for it. (26).

26   Advertisement (detail). Voigtlander Camera. Design: Albert E. Markarian. Kalmar Advertising. Courtesy the designer.

27   William Scrots. *Edward VI.* 1546. Oil on panel, 63 x 16³/₄". Collection National Portrait Gallery, London.

DISTORTION

Certain aberrations and defects of vision can be reproduced to provide a comparable experience for someone with normal vision. These artificially induced distortions or disturbances in the perceptual process are illusions with considerable optical power. Diffused edges may recreate a myopic blur that cannot be resolved. Overlapping multiple images present a problem of selective focus. Repeated information, particularly of facial features, creates a dilemma of attention and number. Even a slight deformation of a familiar subject may suggest impaired vision. Optically stretched images, anamorphic perspective, objects seen through water or glass, and the fun house mirror allow us to share a visual aberration.

An 16th century portrait drawn in anamorphic perspective can be viewed obliquely through a notch in the frame to correct the distortion (27) (28).

28   *Edward VI* viewed in perspective.

2 FINE ARTS

The term "optical" has been used to describe contemporary paintings which are based on perceptual abstractions. These works confront the viewer with a pattern or image that immediately evokes a prescribed visual sensation without the distracting connotations of recognizable subject matter. The vocabulary of painters working within this tradition is derived from those image qualities which produce the strongest retinal experiences. Accidental effects and organic forms are eliminated in favor of geometric clarity. Precise and explicit relationships determine the painting's organization. Refinement and control of edges and surfaces maintain the machine-like precision essential for maximum sensory impact. Choice of scale is a crucial factor in determining the intensity with which the optical effect will be experienced. For this reason perceptual paintings are frequently large enough to dominate the visual field and engulf the viewer in an environment created by the painted surface.

The works included in this section activate vision and demonstrate how intellect and intuition must be combined so that a significant form is evolved from an optical effect.

1   Victor Vasarely. *Helion.* 1960. Oil on canvas, 70 x 47″. Courtesy Galerie Denise René, Paris.

The square and circle have been combined and grouped to create a series of overlapping units with ambiguous figure-ground relationships (1). Closure of form and the use of black and white in approximately equal amounts establish tension in the painting and make it difficult to separate ground from figure.

A positive after-image effect results in an illusion of small grey dots at the intersections of a white grid (2). This illusory dot pattern is restated as a literal part of the composition in a series of scaled black circles. Changes in the size and orientation of the squares produce related spatial effects of compression, expansion, and rotation.

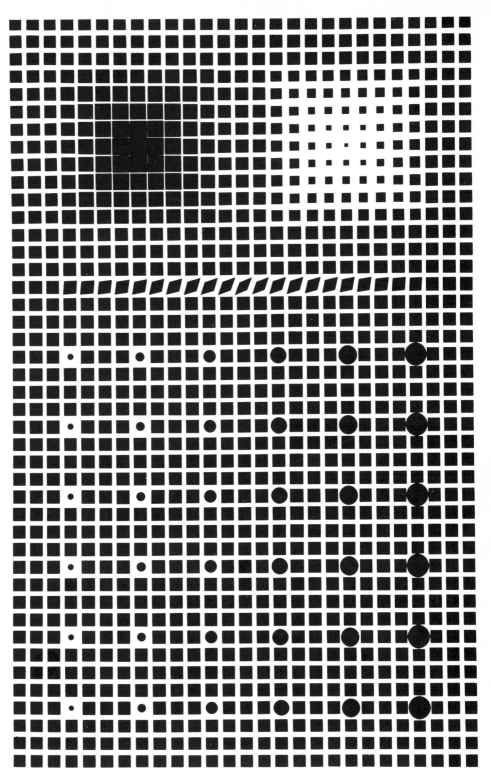

2   Victor Vasarely. *Supernovae*. 1959-61. Oil on canvas, 95 x 138½". Reproduced by Courtesy of the Trustees of the Tate Gallery, London.

3   Victor Vasarely. *Metagalaxie*. 1960-61. Oil on canvas, 58½ x 73½". Courtesy Pace Gallery, New York.

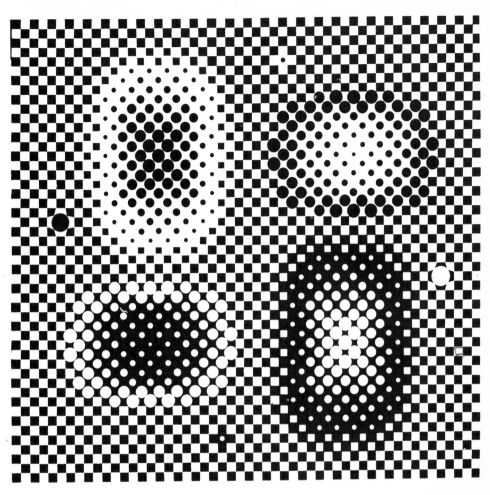

4   Victor Vasarely. *Metagalaxie*. 1959-61. Oil on canvas, 62½ x 57½". Courtesy Galerie Denise René, Paris.

When a particular perceptual effect continues to interest an artist, he may return again and again to the problem of giving new form to the phenomenon. Vasarely has repeatedly explored the conditions which cause the flat two-dimensional surface of a painting to appear to warp, advance, and recede. A checkerboard pattern functions as the basis for two paintings which are similar in intent, but differ radically in form (3) (4).

Progressive elongation of the square units causes two diametrically opposed spatial illusions to occur (3). A diamond-shaped crater appears to recede as a hemisphere apparently bulges forward. A number of smaller pattern shifts and reversals are used to further activate the surface.

A pattern of squares serves as the ground for an image reminiscent of a greatly enlarged halftone dot pattern (4). Square-to-circle transitions and changes in scale create an illusion of raised and recessed areas.

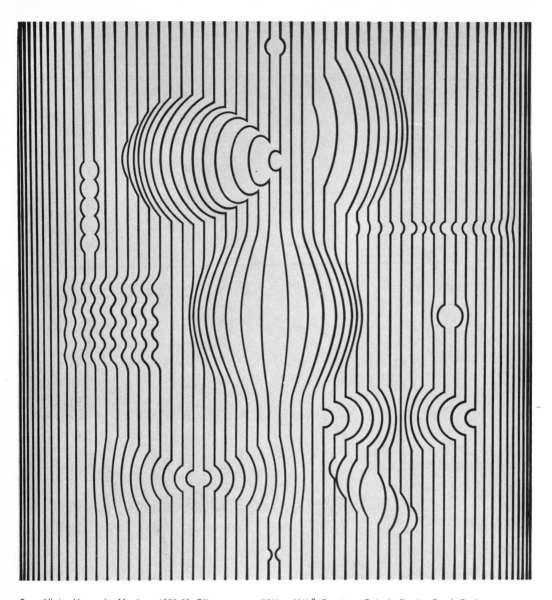

5   Victor Vasarely. *Manipur*. 1952-60. Oil on canvas, 59¹/₂ x 63¹/₂". Courtesy Galerie Denise René, Paris.

6   Victor Vasarely. *Betelgeuse II.* 1958. Oil on canvas, 76³/₄ x 51″. Courtesy Galerie Denise René, Paris.

Distortions in a system of parallel lines create an illusion of three-dimensional topography (5).

Trimming the edges of strategically located circles causes a series of overlapping diamond shapes to separate from the main field of circles (6). The same technique is used to create a subordinate rectangular design. Interruptions in the delineation of the diamond and rectangular patterns heighten the illusion of floating planes.

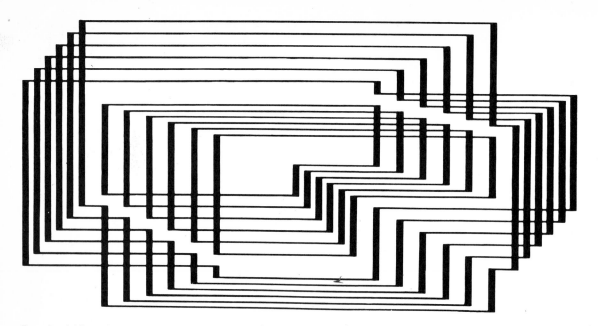

7   Josef Albers. *Interiors.* 1942. Lithograph. Collection Mr. and Mrs. James Fowle, Providence, Rhode Island.

In his teaching and in his art, Josef Albers has consistently explored what he calls "the discrepancy between physical fact and psychic effect." His seemingly rational figures contain the visual cues necessary for two contradictory spatial interpretations. These figures abruptly alter their position in space as our attention shifts from one set of cues to the other (7) (8) (9). Our fascination with this ambiguity grows as we try to resolve the discrepancy and determine the means used by the artist to create the figure.

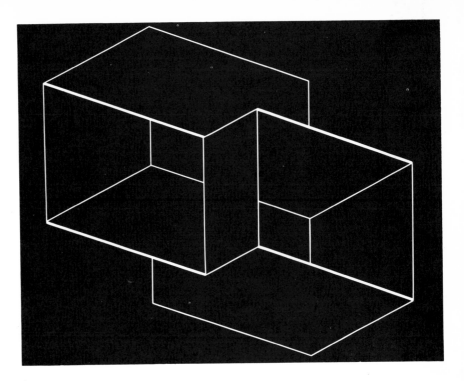

8

9

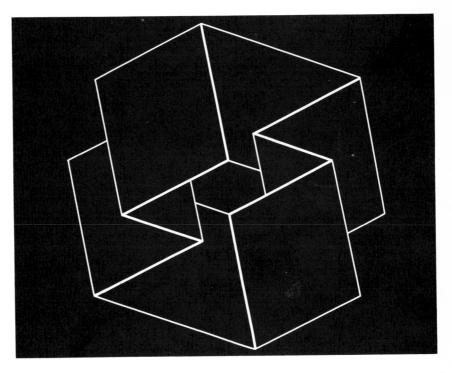

(8) (9)   Josef Albers. "Structural Constellations." 1953-58. *Despite Straight Lines*, pages 63, 79. Courtesy the artist.

10   Bridget Riley. *Disturbance*. 1964. Emulsion on board, 68 x 68". Collection Mr. and Mrs. Albert List, Byrum, Conn. Courtesy Richard Feigen Gallery, New York.

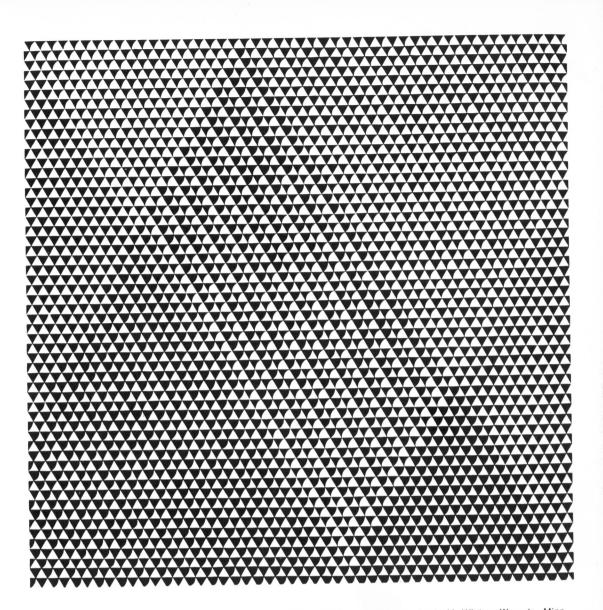

11   Bridget Riley. *Tremor*. 1962. Emulsion on board, 46⅝ x 48⅛". Collection Mr. David M. Winton, Wayzata, Minn. Courtesy Richard Feigen Gallery, New York.

Geometric units establish a periodic pattern that can be transformed and intensified by varying the size, shape, and placement of the basic unit (10) (11). As the eye focuses on specific parts of the pattern, the isolation of an area produces a temporary stability and sense of order. Secondary forms emerge as the black and white contrast fatigues the eye and forces one image to overlap another. Optimum sensory impact depends upon the scale of the individual units and the size of the actual canvas. If the reproductions are held uncomfortably close to the eyes, the quality of the originals will be more nearly approximated.

12   Bridget Riley. *Interrupted Circle*. 1963. Emulsion on board, 45³/₄ x 46³/₈". Collection Mr. and Mrs. Harold Strauss, Chicago. Courtesy Richard Feigen Gallery, New York.

13   Bridget Riley. *Blaze 4*. 1963. Emulsion on board, 37¼ x 37¼". Collection Mrs. Louise Riley, London. Courtesy Richard Feigen Gallery, New York.

A format of distorted concentric circles has been divided into three sections (12). Oblique straight lines connect the sections and suggest a series of ambiguous spatial separations.

A diagonal stripe pattern has been applied to the surface of a series of eccentric circles to produce a figure of unusual spatial properties (13). The stripes reverse in direction and alternate in value causing the circular divisions to read as folded ridges.

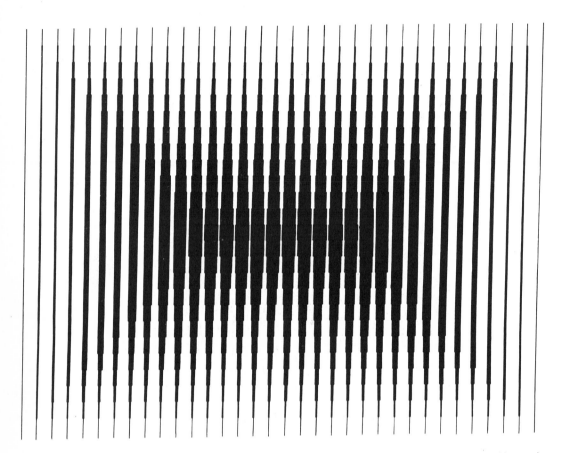

14   Jeffrey Steele. *Gespenstische Gestalt.* 1961. Oil on canvas, 27 x 36″. Collection Walker Art Gallery, Liverpool. Courtesy Grabowski Gallery, London.

Dark areas are most frequently interpreted as being spatially more distant than white or light areas (14). Reordering the gradient pattern causes a reversal of this relationship (15).

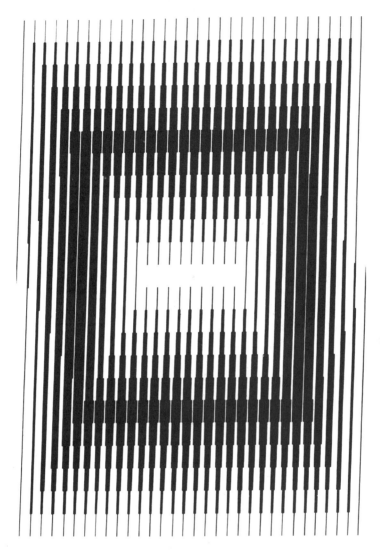

15   Jeffrey Steele. *Divertissement*. 1963. Gouache, 25 x 18". Courtesy Grabowski Gallery, London.

16   Jeffrey Steele. *Baroque Experiment: Fred Maddox*. 1964. Oil on canvas, 60 x 40". Collection Hon. Anthony Samuel. Courtesy Grabowski Gallery, London.

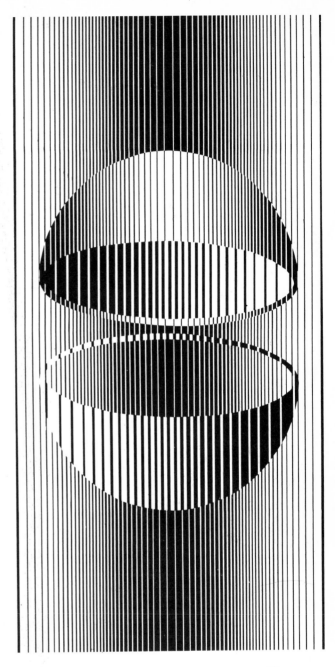

17   Ronald G. Carraher. *Conics*. 1965. Serigraph, 12 x 19".

The visualization of an "endless" space can be achieved
with mathematical progressions (16). Fascination with
this form is related to gradient patterns and the role such
unit structures have in creating an illusion of the third
dimension. A bowl shape within a system of graduated
lines is inverted and reversed to suggest both a solid
and a void (17).

18   Reginald Neal. *Square of Three*. 1964. Litho and paint on canvas, 32 x 32". Courtesy Amel Gallery, New York.

19   Richard Anuszkiewicz. *Division of Intensity*. 1964. Acrylic on board, 48 x 48″. Courtesy Martha Jackson Gallery, New York.

A number of illusions may be produced by placing geometric figures in an environment composed of strong directional or spatial elements. Converging lines warp the parallel sides of contained squares (18) (19).

20   Francois Morellet. *Screen Painting: 0°, 22°5, 45°, 67°5.* 1958. Oil on canvas, 55⅛ x 55⅛". Courtesy The Contemporaries, New York.

21   Francois Morellet. *Tirets: 0°-90°*. 1960. Oil on canvas, 55 x 55″. Collection Jack Youngerman. Courtesy The Contemporaries, New York.

Intersecting grids of lines produce delicate secondary circular shapes that vary only slightly in their size and form (20). As the surface of the painting is studied, these circles seem to flicker, disappear, and then reappear. The nature of the illusion may rest with the inability of the eye to sustain a sense impression or to remain fixed on one part of the pattern.

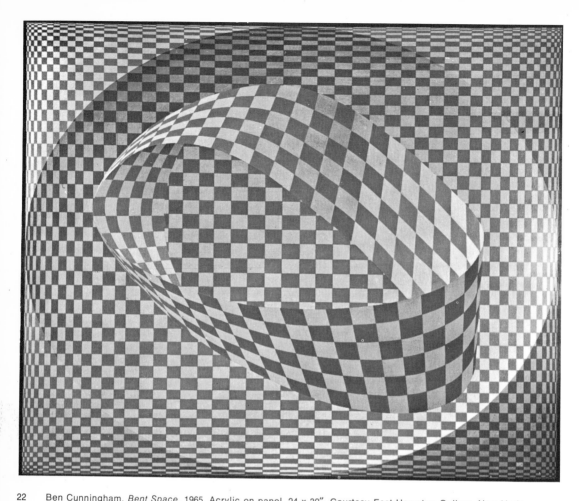

22   Ben Cunningham. *Bent Space*. 1965. Acrylic on panel, 24 x 30". Courtesy East-Hampton Gallery, New York.

Checkerboard units have been altered so that they describe a mobius strip suspended in a concave ellipse (22). Changing the scale and orientation of the squares causes the figure to float in front of the background. Convergence of the pattern makes the corners of the painting appear to bend away from the viewer.

Marcel Duchamp's "Roto-Reliefs" are designed to be viewed as they rotate on a record turntable. In motion the circle patterns seem to shift position on the disc and assume three-dimensional properties (23) (24).

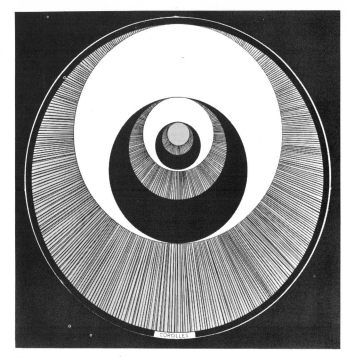

23

24

(23) Marcel Duchamp. *Corolles*.

(24) Marcel Duchamp. *Lanterne Chinoise*.

From *12 Rotoreliefs* set of 6 discs with design on either side to be seen in revolution. Offset lithograph, printed in color 7⅞″ diam. Study collection, The Museum of Modern Art, New York. Gift of Rose Fried.

25   Norman Ives. *D-P Diagonal*. 1964. Ink on paper on masonite, 30 x 48". Collection
      Mr. Malcolm Grear, Providence, Rhode Island.

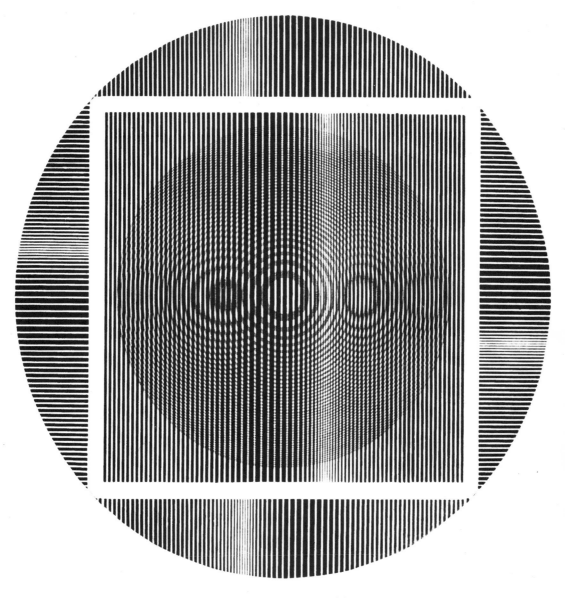

26   Reginald Neal. *Red, White & Black Round.* 1964. Litho and ink, 18″ diam. Courtesy Amel Gallery, New York.

Letterforms have been cut into units and arranged to equalize surface activity (25). Aligned edges create a series of diagonals, forcing elusive diamond-shaped planes to separate from the surface. The dynamic balance of black and white causes a reversible figure-ground illusion.

Horizontal lines and a system of concentric circles are overlapped to produce a grouping of moiré effects (26).

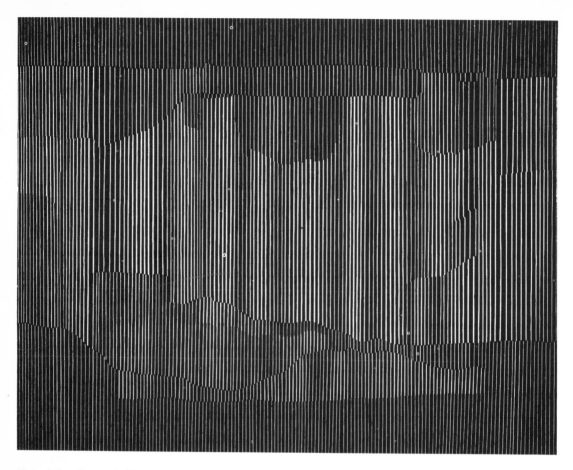

27   Julian Stanczak. *Nocturnal Interlude*. 1964. Acrylic on canvas, 54½ x 69½". Courtesy Martha Jackson Gallery, New York.

Mathematical models or systems often inspire as well as actually assist the artist in achieving a particular optical effect. A figure constructed entirely of straight lines contains an illusion of spiraling, curved planes (28).

28   Franco Grignani. *Tridimensionabilità Strutturale*. 1965. Oil on canvas, 37½ x 30". Courtesy the artist.

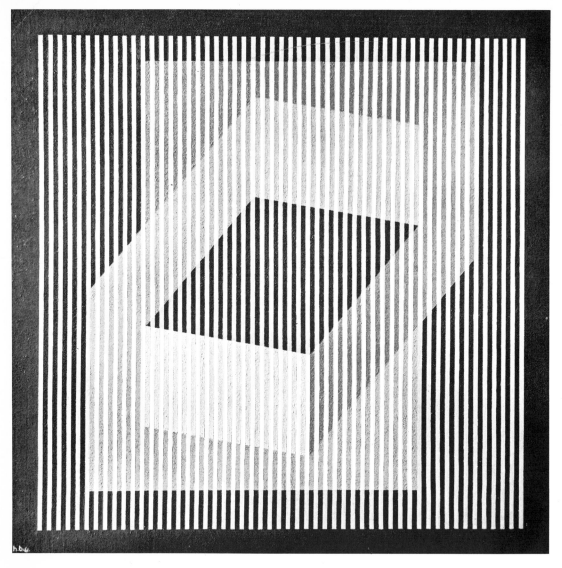

29   Hannes Beckmann. *Neither Nor*. 1961. Oil, 30 x 30″. Collection Boston Museum of Fine Arts, Boston, Massachusetts.

30   Spencer Moseley. *Little Portuguese Bend*. 1966. Acrylic on canvas, 40 x 40". Courtesy the artist.

3   PHOTOGRAPHY

The role of an optical effect in a photograph must be understood in terms of the photographer's intention. The effect may be the primary interest of the photographer or it may be the formal means he has chosen to visualize and dramatize a more complex idea. The illusion is often the product of a unique moment in which a series of visual elements coincides to create a special effect. The photographer selects and isolates this information for the final print. He may amplify certain qualities by manipulating various photographic variables such as exposure, selective focus, and tonal range. The optical illusion may exist in nature or it may be the product of experimentation with the photographic process. Images may be physically overlapped through multiple exposure to produce ambiguities of form and space.

1   Margaret Bourke-White. *Contour Plowing*. 1954. Courtesy Life magazine.

2   Joseph Jachna. *Coal Pile*. 1964. Courtesy the photographer.

The sweeping pattern created by contour plowing appears to undulate and separate from the landscape (1). The fluctuation of the plowed band makes alternate spatial readings possible.

Nearly equal areas of white and black are opposed in a photograph of a coal field partially covered with snow. The symmetrical arrangement and similarity of value between the sky and snow make it difficult to establish a constant spatial relationship for the areas of white, grey, and black (2).

3   Peter Thomann. *Oriental Alley*. 1964. (First Prize, World Press Exhibition). Courtesy the photographer.

4   Peter Thomann. *Nursing Zebra*. 1964. Courtesy the photographer.

Merging zebra stripe patterns obscure the identity of the animals. The viewer responds to the tension and contrast of the stripes as an experience apart from the pictorial subject (4).

An overhead lattice separates sunlight into vertical bands which illuminate a crowded alley (3). The interrupted light source superimposes a high contrast gradient pattern on the robed figures. A spatial progression is defined by changes in the width of the stripes.

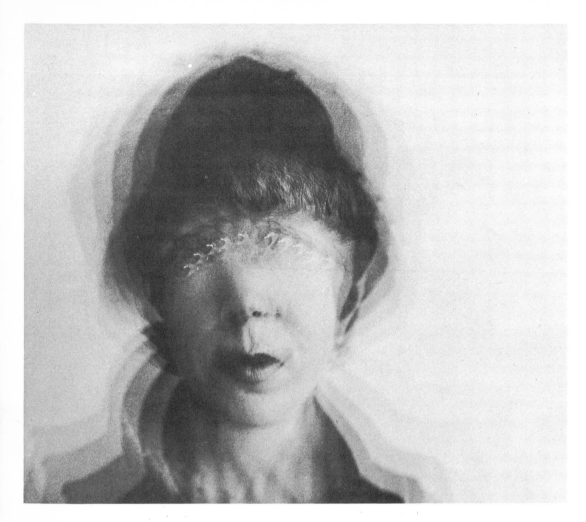

5   Sam Smidt. *Shirley Coates*. 1965. Courtesy the photographer.

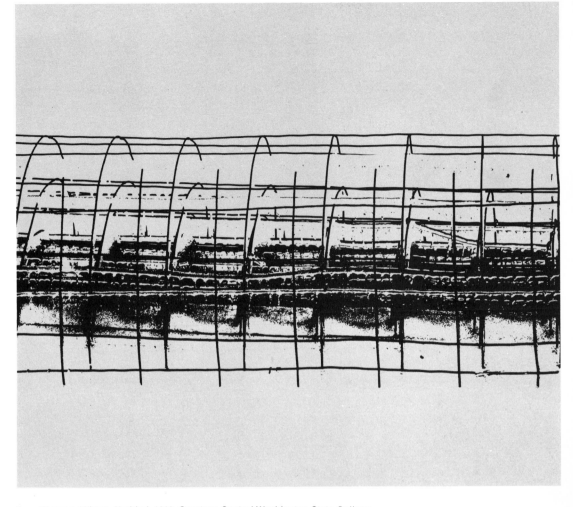

6   Richard Allison. *Untitled.* 1962. Courtesy Central Washington State College.

Multiple exposures of the same subject were made by progressively tilting the camera (5). The effect of controlled blurring induces a strong illusion of movement.

A roll of wire in the snow has been photographed on high contrast film to emphasize its linear pattern (6). Icicles and the snow add textural interest; but an illusion of spatial ambiguity allows us to interpret the rolled wire units as bending toward the foreground or away from the picture plane.

4 GRAPHIC DESIGN

Because optical illusions and perceptual effects have the power to evoke an immediate and predictable sensation, they provide the designer with an important resource. The optical illusion may engage the observer on a purely sensory level or it may be used to create a unique connection between verbal and visual meanings. Innovations with optical effects retain the clarity, economy, and precision that characterize contemporary design. Designs which evolve from a perceptual effect are an "art of the essential" with each visual element a carefully considered component of the final statement. The works reproduced in this section illustrate how the inherent interest and form of the optical illusion may be used to realize the objectives of the graphic designer.

The photo-reproduction methods utilized in the graphic arts provide controls that are particularly suited for the production of some of the more complex optical effects. At the designer's disposal are such technical means as the distortion camera and special effect halftone screens. Methods of presentation range from the printed page to the projected image of the animated film.

Many ideas which originate in the fine arts ultimately find application in graphic design statements, and original research by the graphic designer generates information which may in turn have an effect upon the fine arts.

1   Optical experiments. Design: Franco Grignani. Courtesy the designer.

The artist working with applications of optical effects must often conduct considerable research in evolving new forms and techniques (1). The photographic process provides a valuable tool for such experimentation. Original designs may be optically transformed into expanding radial patterns as they are reflected onto warped surfaces. Delicate details contribute to a strong illusion of three-dimensional topography.

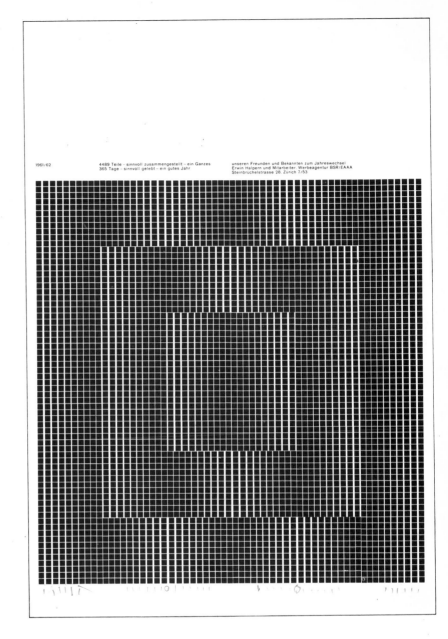

1961/62   4489 Teile - sinnvoll zusammengestellt - ein Ganzes   unseren Freunden und Bekannten zum Jahreswechsel
365 Tage - sinnvoll gelebt - ein gutes Jahr   Erwin Halpern und Mitarbeiter. Werbeagentur BSR/EAAA
Steinbruchstrasse 28. Zürich 7/53

2   New Year's card. Design: Fridolin Muller. Courtesy Erwin Halpern Advertising Agency, Zurich, Switzerland.

Periodic increases in the weight of the verticals make
the surface of a grid of squares appear to undulate (2).
An additional sense of space is achieved by interrupting
the vertical alignment.

3   Advertisement (detail). Alfieri and Lacroix. Design: Franco Grignani. Courtesy the designer.

Familiar forms of the infinite progression and the spiral are rephrased by a series of figure-ground shapes (3) (4). The eye is repeatedly compelled to follow the same path to the center of the vortex. Popularity of the spiral as a decorative motif challenges the designer to create a fresh variation and to place it in a new context.

4   Folder. Kromekote Paper. Design: Rolf Harder. Courtesy the designer.

Resochin

chlorochini
phosphas NFN
til behandling
af lysdermatiter

5

(5) (6) Brochure covers. Bayer AG. Design: Graphikteam (Hans Buschfeld, Siegfried Himmer, Winfried Holtz, Heinz Lippert, Coordt von Mannstein). Courtesy the designers.

Trenimon® Cytostatique

Action instantanée	Action intense	Action locale	Présentation
indispensable pour assurer la prévention pré, per et postopératoire des métastases	traitement d'entretien per os, notamment aussi en cas d'hémoblastoses, par seulement 1 à 3 capsules à 0,5 mg **par semaine**	en cas d'épanchements pleuraux et péritonéaux d'origine cancéreuse	5 ampoules à 0,2 mg de substance sèche,10 et 30 capsules à 0,5 mg

6

At optimum viewing distance the serrated edges of the chevrons begin to blur as the eye strains to accommodate itself to the indistinct form (6). This diffusion effect can be used to create a strong illusion of vibration or implied movement (5).

7

8

Gradients of varying intervals and weight combine to create illusions of space and form (7) (8). What appears to be an opening in a sphere may also be perceived as an advancing suspended circle.

(7) (8) Collages from the book *15 Constellations* by Rob S. Gessner and Eugen Gomringen. Designs: Rob S. Gessner. Courtesy the designer.

9   Poster (detail). School of Visual Arts. Design: Milton Glaser. Photograph: Sol Mednick. Courtesy the designer.

10   From the jacket of *SELF-CREATIONS: 13 Impersonalities* by Thomas B. Morgan, published by Holt, Rinehart and Winston, Inc. Design: Milton Glaser. Photograph: Sol Mednick.

The visual paradox is frequently used by graphic designers to create an image which will arrest the viewer's attention. Familiar subjects may be juxtaposed or actually joined to communicate a new meaning (9) (10).

Ballungen

rlerbert W. Kapitzki

Die Welt ist kleiner geworden,
die Menschheit rückt zusammen.
Aus vielen Einzelnen werden Gruppen,
Verbände, Massen.
Massen, die in Bewegung geraten,
Massen, die den Einzelnen mitreißen.
Deshalb ist es wichtig,
einen Standpunkt zu haben,
sich zu orientieren
und täglich neu zu informieren.
Darum ist es richtig, sie täglich zu lesen:
Stuttgarter Nachrichten.   Immer lesenswert · immer aktuell

Stuttgarter Nachrichten   unabhängig überparteilich fortschrittlich

11   Advertisement. *Stuttgarter Nachrichten*. Design: Herbert Kapitzki. Courtesy the designer.

12   Optical study. Design: Herbert Kapitzki. Courtesy the designer.

A German newspaper advertisement succinctly visualizes for the reader the concept of a crowd (11). The small concave triangular units are joined to produce both a symbol and an unusual figure-ground pattern.

A grid of squares has been modified to create a triangular pattern (12). Further sequential changes in the triangles produce a sense of tilted planes and shifting currents. The black fragments merge in a single perceptual event. .

13   Symbol. (Hotel). Design: Norman Ives. Courtesy the designer.

14   Symbol. Brown University Press. Design: Malcolm Grear. Courtesy the designer.

TRADEMARK DESIGN

The visual forms that provide the basis for many optical illusions are of particular value to the graphic designer concerned with creating a trademark or corporate symbol. An effective trademark is a distinctive and memorable symbol for the company it represents. The design may also communicate something about the business activity of the firm. This combination of qualities must be achieved with forms that will retain their clarity when reproduced either as enlarged or greatly reduced versions. Such limitations are seldom more effectively resolved than when the trademark incorporates the impact and pleasure of a perceptual illusion.

The architectural form of the hotel symbol contains contradictory visual cues which result in two possible spatial readings of the letter *H* (13). The activity of the figure is sustained by this alternation.

The Brown University colophon elegantly integrates a number of visual objectives (14). The letterform *B* is used to construct a stack of books which symbolizes the function of a press. Equal bands of black and white describe the pages of the books and activate a reversible figure that occupies two contradictory spatial positions.

15

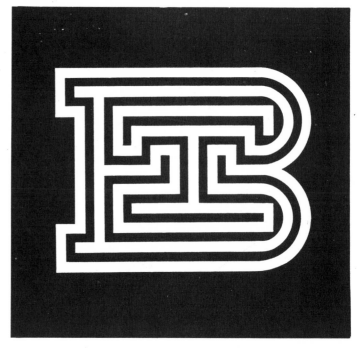

16

(15) Symbol. Bay State Abrasives. Design: Malcolm Grear. Courtesy the designer.
(16) Symbol. (Bank). Design: Norman Ives. Courtesy the designer.
(17) Symbol. Howell Design Associates. Design: Malcolm Grear. Courtesy the designer.

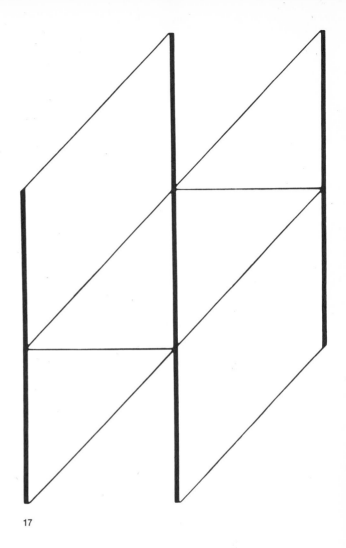

17

Two sets of circles have been arranged to suggest the letter *B* and a pair of grinding wheels (15). By reversing the values of the two circles the designer has introduced an illusion of space and movement without altering the clarity of the symbol.

One of the difficulties of combining letterforms in trademark design is organizing the visual statement so that the letters will be read in proper sequence. The interlocking geometric pattern of the meander or Greek key pattern establishes the format for this trademark in which the letter order has been carefully determined (16). *B* is read before *T* because of its dominant silhouette. *T* follows as a consequence of the figure-ground movement of the equal bands of light and dark.

The increased width of the verticals simultaneously defines the edges of parallel planes and contributes to the spatial ambiguity of the figure (17). Both the name of the firm and its interior design services are represented by the symbol.

18

19

20

(18) Symbol. Color Concentrate Corporation. Design: Malcolm Grear. Courtesy the designer.

(19) Symbol. Research & Design, Inc. Design: Malcolm Grear. Courtesy the designer.

(20) Symbol. Rugoff Theatres. Design: Norman Ives. Courtesy the designer.

21   Symbol. Merrimack Valley Textile Museum. Design: Malcolm Grear. Courtesy the designer.

The triangular format traditionally used to signify the primary colors has been created by grouping the initials of the firm (18). Negative space enclosed by the letters becomes a fluctuating figure-ground shape.

Letterforms have been arranged to imply either the interior or the exterior of a three-dimensional cube (19). Figure-ground alternation results from placing the interlocking r and d in equal areas.

An illusion of three-dimensional space emerges as a section of a single letterform economically serves a dual purpose (20). Repetition of this carefully designed shape around a center point establishes spatial cues and recreates the original letter. The verbal and visual logic of the symbol are so fused that it is difficult to experience one of the letters without reading the next.

An illusion of advancing and receding space is created by reversed gradient forms of the letter T (21). The interlocking linear pattern also provides a visual reference to the weaving process of the textile industry.

5 VISUAL CONUNDRUMS AND THE NON-RATIONAL

The visual conundrum constitutes a special category of illusion quite unlike the perceptual abstractions considered thus far. The conundrum is traditionally a puzzling question or riddle based upon a fantastic resemblance between things which are quite unlike. Representational art describes subject matter by means of conventions which comprise a kind of visual logic. These forms of representation can be manipulated to create contradictions or to phrase visual questions. The illusions emerge as deliberate discrepancies in the painting's continuity. Because we anticipate a consistent presentation of the subject we are disconcerted by the presence of non-rational elements. Contradictory visual perceptions are not easily comprehended simultaneously. One interpretation may be exchanged for another, but only one can be verified at a given moment. This alternation between literal meanings can be considered as a counterpart of the reversible geometric figures considered earlier. The conundrum thus becomes a play upon our educated vision.

1 René Magritte. *Les Promenades d'Euclide*. 1955. Oil, 63½ x 51½". Collection Alexander Iolas Gallery, New York, Paris, Geneva.

2   René Magritte. *La Cascade.* 1961. Oil, 32 x 39½". Collection Alexander Iolas Gallery, New York, Paris, Geneva.

The paintings of René Magritte explore the tradition of conundrums and incongruities. The frame within a frame of "La Cascade" disappoints our expectation that the painting on the easel will be less naturalistic than the leaves that surround it (2). The inner painting belongs to the foreground, but it can also be interpreted as a window overlooking a more distant forest.

The tower roof and empty street in "Les Promenades d'Euclide" are rendered as interchangeable experiences (1). Since a solid cone can also be seen as a flat plane in perspective, the viewer is forced to suspend belief in the logic of the painting as he attempts to resolve an improbable visual coincidence.

3 René Magritte. *Le Choeur des Sphynges*. 1964. Gouache. 13½ x 21". Collection Alexander Iolas Gallery, New York, Paris, Geneva.

The foliage shapes in "Le Choeur des Sphynges" float cloudlike above the landscape and may be experienced either as superimposed forms or as openings in the sky (3). This dual spatial function creates a figure-ground illusion. Constructing both landscape and clouds from a common foliage pattern establishes a correlation between unlike objects and further complicates the meaning of the floating shapes.

4   M. C. Escher. *Relativity*. 1953. Lithograph. Courtesy Mickelson Gallery, Washington, D.C.

Certain mental images and ideas are best understood in visual form. In the print "Relativity" humanoids and pieces of furniture are used as props to establish three independent but intersecting worlds (4). One consistent system of perspective creates an interior that houses these three worlds and their gravitational fields. A horizontal plane for one inhabitant becomes a vertical plane for another.

5   Salvador Dali. *Slave Market with Disappearing Bust of Voltaire.* 1940. Oil on canvas, 18¹/₄ x 25³/₄". Collection The Reynolds Morse Foundation.

A new level of comprehension is reached when initially perceived information is transformed by the discovery of a concealed image. The viewer participates in the process of organizing the new information into its various possible combinations. In "Slave Market with Disappearing Bust of Voltaire" by Salvador Dali, the head of Voltaire and the two coifed nuns have been subtly altered so that the perception of one depends upon the presence of the other (5). Although the figures are imbedded within the same contour, it is difficult to experience them simultaneously.

Salvador Dali. Study for *Slave Market with Disappearing Bust of Voltaire* (detail).

6   Salvador Dali. *The Three Ages*. 1940. Oil on canvas, 19⅝ x 25⅝". Collection The Reynolds Morse Foundation.

Dali employs his "paranoic-critical method" to relate a succession of images within images. An intricate chain of associations based on combinations of landscape, masonry and figures symbolizes the evolution from youth to old age (6).

Salvador Dali. *Skull of Zurbaran.* 1956. Oil on canvas, 39½ x 39½″. Collection Joseph H. Hirshhorn Foundation, New York.

6 FOR THE STUDENT

An introduction to the various optical effects and related perceptual processes provides the art student with a visual vocabulary and method of problem solving. As the student works he must continually evaluate and reflect upon his own visual process as a means of testing the effectiveness of his ideas. Involvement with a seemingly simple form must persist until discoveries can be refined and controlled as part of a consistent idea. The quality and power of the finished design depends upon craftsmanship and an applied understanding of the principles of optical effects. Because of the contemporary importance of perceptual abstraction and the historical precedents for its forms, investigation of this subject is of value to the art student.

1

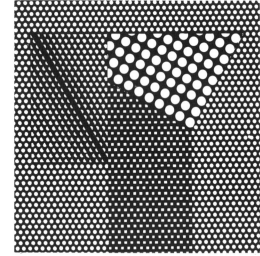

2

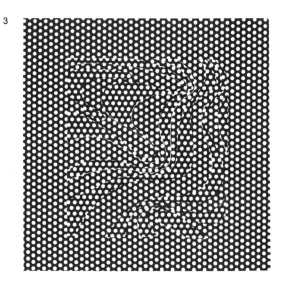

3

4

Specific optical effects provide a creative focus for student projects. The student work reproduced in this section reveals the variety of possibilities which may be developed within the limitations of a single concept. A periodic pattern of white dots silk-screened on a black background serves as the basis for a number of perceptual statements (1) (2) (3) (4). Altering the dot size, superimposing secondary patterns, and regrouping the dots are some of the techniques employed by the students to modify the original pattern and create the resulting illusions of space and form.

(1) (2) (3) (4) Student projects. Instructor R. Carraher. Art Department, San Jose State College.

5

6

(5)   Student project. Record album jacket.
(7)   Student project. Symbol for coffee syrup product.
(6) (8) Student projects. Exercise using ruling pens.

Student projects. Instructor Malcolm Grear. Graphic Design Department, Rhode Island School of Design.

7

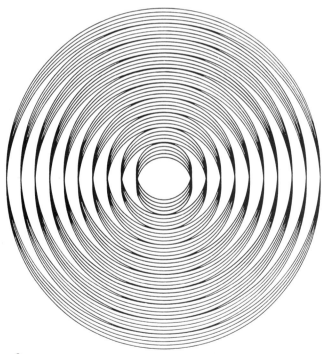

8

Linear systems created with ruling pen and compass can be combined, interrupted, and ordered to produce effects that range from moiré patterns to reversible figures (6) (8).

9

10

11

(9) (10) (11) Student projects. Perceptual pat-
terns developed from a square grid. Instructor
Jacqueline B. Thurston. Art Department, San
Jose State College.

GLOSSARY OF OPTICAL ILLUSIONS

This final section consists of a visual glossary of optical illusions and figures which demonstrate perceptual effects. The examples have been grouped on the basis of similarity of effect and are accompanied by brief verbal descriptions of the particular properties of each figure. Theoretical discussion is impractical in this context since scientific research does not yet provide a consistent explanation for many aspects of the perceptual process. The glossary figures isolate effects that are incorporated in many of the paintings and graphic designs presented in the previous sections. These figures also provide a resource for the artist interested in further investigation of the subject.

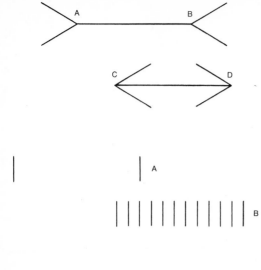

The Müller-Lyer illusion. Although line **AB** appears to be longer than line **CD**, the two horizontals are equal.

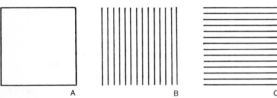

The undivided space of **A** appears smaller than the divided space of **B.***

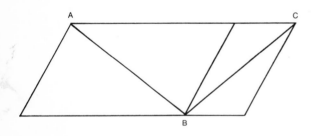

Three identical squares appear unequal because divided space seems to occupy a larger area than undivided space. The directional orientation of the space divisions further distorts the proportions of the original square.

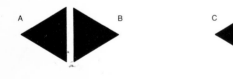

Two parallelograms contain diagonals of equal length. The larger parallelogram is divided by line **AB** which seems longer than line **BC.**

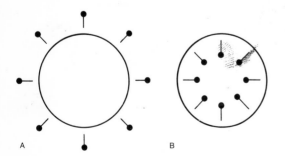

Although point **B** lies midway between points **A** and **C,** the distance from **B** to **C** seems greater.

Although circles **A** and **B** are identical, circle **B** seems smaller. The subdivisions within circle **B** create a sense of contraction, while the same pattern placed outside the circumference of circle **A** creates a sense of expansion.*

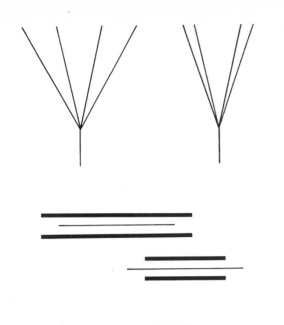

The interior angles of these two figures are equal. They appear unequal because they are flanked by two sets of angles which differ in size.*

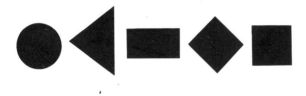

The contrasting lengths of the two sets of black bars cause the equal center lines to appear disproportionate.

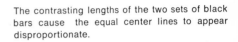

Two identical white center sections appear unequal because of the contrasting lengths of the adjacent black segments.

Angles and contrasting shapes make these five equal areas appear unequal.*

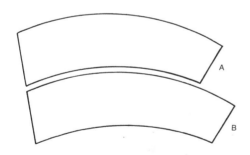

Juxtaposing the smaller arc of **A** to the larger arc of **B** makes the upper figure seem smaller. Both figures are the same size.

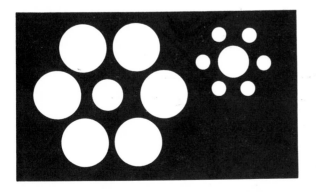

The equal center circles seem to be unequal because of the contrasting scale of the outer circles.

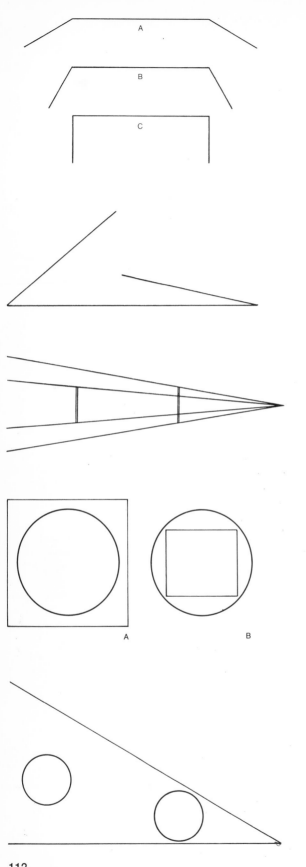

The three horizontal lines **A, B,** and **C** seem to be of different lengths. The angles created by the attached lines affect the apparent length of the horizontals.

Two equal oblique lines appear unequal because of the difference in their distance from the base line.

Two vertical lines of equal length appear unequal because of their position within contrasting angles.

The circles in figures **A** and **B** are the same size although the circle enclosing the square appears smaller.

Two circles of the same size appear unequal because of their position within an angle. The circle nearest the apex of the angle seems larger.

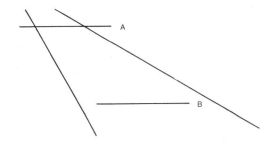

Converging lines make line **A** seem longer than line **B** and create an illusion in perspective.

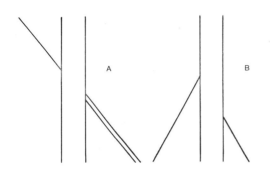

The vertical lines in figure **A** make it difficult to identify the true continuation of the interrupted diagonal. Contrary to most estimates, the diagonals of figure **B** would meet on the left. This is known as "Poggendorf's illusion."

Another illusion in perspective occurs when three identical repetitions of a human figure appear to increase in scale. This discrepancy between actual height and apparent height depends on the figure's location in a system of converging lines.

SSSSS
8888888
SSSSS
8888888

Some letterforms and numerals must be proportioned to avoid a top heavy appearance. When these figures are inverted, their disparity in form becomes immediately apparent.

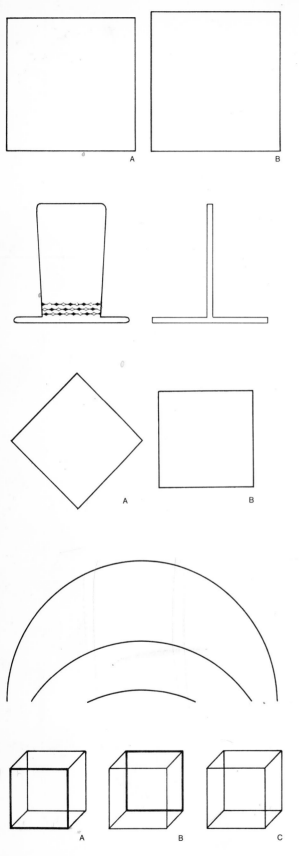

A correctly drawn square **B** appears too tall. A slightly shorter rectangle **A** seems to be a perfect square.

Verticals generally appear to be greater in length than horizontals of the same size.

A square seems larger when tilted on one corner and viewed as a diamond shape.

Changes in size make arcs of the same circle appear to vary in curvature. *

Figures **A** and **B** illustrate the two alternate spatial interpretations for figure **C** and demonstrate how cubes can be reversed.

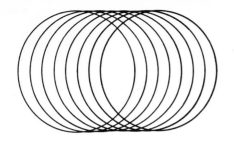

Either side of this series of rings may be seen as the near or far end of a tube. These are reversible circles.

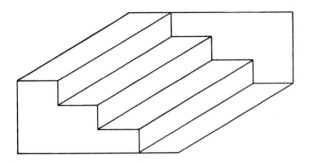

"Schröder's reversible staircase."

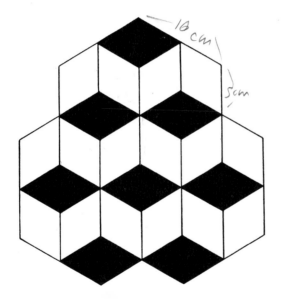

It is possible to count six or seven stacked cubes, depending on whether the black diamonds are viewed as the tops or bottoms of the cubes.

A

B

A pattern of short cross strokes causes parallel lines to apparently bend. Any given pair of parallel lines will seem to diverge in the direction that the cross strokes converge.

The same pair of eyes appears to look in opposite directions. A change in the orientation of the lower portion of the face causes this apparent shift in direction of vision. The illusion is destroyed if the lower halves of both faces are covered.

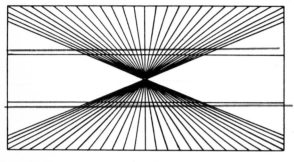

"Hering's illusion of direction" is shown in this example. Although the horizontal lines are parallel, they appear to bow apart in the middle, opposite the point of convergence.

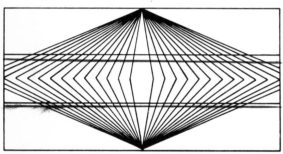

When the points of convergence lie outside the parallel lines, we have an example of "Wundt's illusion of direction," as the lines appear to diverge when they reach the sides of the figure.

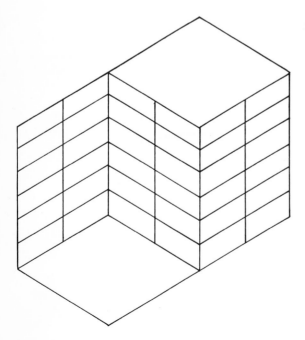

This equivocal figure may appear to exist either above or below the viewer's eye level, and is known as "Thiery's figure."

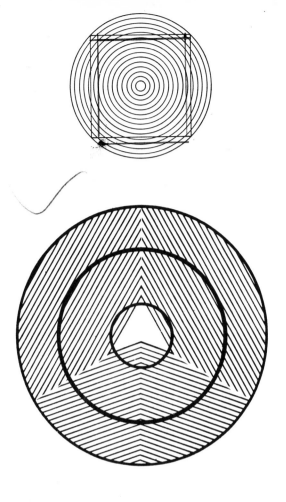

A pattern of concentric circles causes the sides of a square to appear to bow in toward the center of the figure.

A background pattern of diagonal lines causes the superimposed circles to appear distorted.*

The directional power of the background pattern forces the eye to focus on the center of this figure, which is based on a variation of the "Frazer Spiral." True circles are misread as distorted spirals.

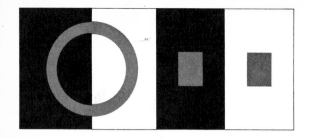

Although the grey circle and both grey rectangles are identical in value, the rectangle set against a white field appears darker.

Irradiation effect. The white square appears larger than the black square of equal size.

Illusory grey spots appear at the points of intersection of a black and a white grid. The effect does not occur at the specific intersection on which the viewer focuses.

An illusion of elusive grey pie shapes on the
surface of a pattern of concentric circles causes
the figure to appear to turn.

When rotated, spirals appear to expand or con-
tract depending upon the direction of rotation.
The constantly changing position of the curved
elements contributes to the illusion.

A variation on the spiral pattern.

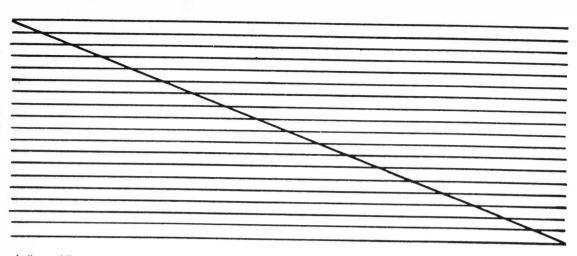

A diagonal line appears to twist in and out of a grid of horizontal lines. The points of intersection modulate the thickness of the diagonal. This figure demonstrates the moiré phenomenon in its simplest form.

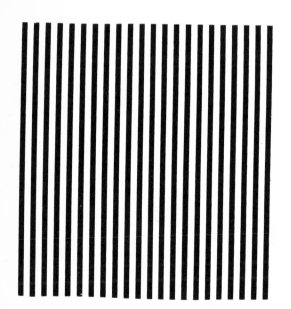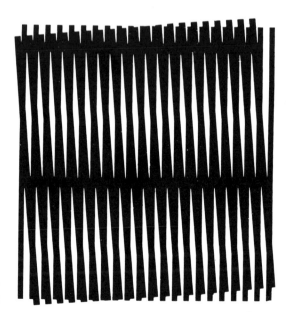

A periodic structure superimposed on itself at a slight angle will produce a moiré pattern.

The meander or Greek key is a variation of the
figure-ground pattern. It may be read as white
lines on a black background or as black lines on
a white background.

When certain visual cues are removed it becomes difficult for the viewer to achieve closure. Individuals vary in the amount of time they require to identify the original subject of these test patterns.

Closure figure of a horse and rider.**

Closure figure of a dog.**

Closure figure of a kneeling man.**

The narrow spacing between the letterforms of a 19th-century wooden type face creates a figure-ground alternation and vibration.

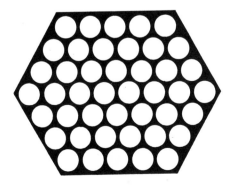

Concentrated study of this figure causes the circles to appear hexagonal in character. Prolonged viewing also causes triangular, hexagonal, and rhomboid groupings of the circles to emerge.*

Repetitions of the same figure scaled to fit within itself suggest the illusion of an infinite progression.

An irrational figure.

Duplication of facial features such as the eyes or mouth creates a conflict of grouping since it is difficult to logically resolve the repetitions.

CREDITS

• Indicates glossary illustrations from M. Luckiesh. *Visual Illusions.* Princeton, N. J.: D. Van Nostrand Company, Inc., 1922.

•• Indicates illustrations from R. F. Street, "Gestalt Completion Test," 1931. *Teachers College Contributions to Education* 481. Bureau of Publications, Teachers College, Columbia University.

Moiré patterns (page 17) produced with Moiré Kit of Edmund Scientific Co., Barrington, New Jersey.